STRAND FULTON STREET.

Diaghilev's Debrief

By
Portia Franco

Chatterley Press International

19 Dorothy Street, Port Jefferson, NY 11776

Diaghilev's Debrief; edited by Christina Tumminello. Copyright 2005 by Christina Tumminello, Chatterley Press International. All rights reserved.

Table of Contents, Publisher's Preface, Recommended Reading List, About The Author by Christina Tumminello, Copyright 2005, Chatterley Press International. All Rights Reserved.

Chatterley Press International
19 Dorothy Street
Port Jefferson, NY 11776 U.S.A.

For information visit our website *www.chatterleypress.com*

Cover Photograph from "A Ballerina Prepares" copyright Lisa Raymond.
For more information visit the artist's website www.lisa-raymond.com

Cover design/layout, and interior design/layout by Christina Tumminello.

First Edition. Printed in the United States of America.
ISBN 0-9713363-8-5
LCCN 2005936922

Dedication

For my family.

Table Of Contents

Diaghilev's Debrief

A Ballerina Prepares

Before I danced, I was me—I think—
Or was there a me without
the tendus punishing my toes?

The insides of my legs,
TURNOUT—"What kind of dancer are you?"
Contort all the way and remember to

breathe—deeply, ribs cracking for air,
again, and again, for the will
is creeping and building in the sublime reaches

of a liquid place,
invisible and unseen.
It is the calling. "Merci Monsieur Diaghilev."

It is the voice that says "I am"—
His stare, Diaghilev's seduction,
anointing Nijinsky, it poisons

my willing mind—my
unwilling flesh that begs for more—exhale—
to move wildly and to live elsewhere

in frenzy, beyond the pain, beyond the
wanting and the need—the sweat, under pink
stockings. The agitation breathes and burrows

In the wool that wraps my feet.
It comforts me—when I'm alone—exhausted

and breathing, gasping

for more—my addiction, my jolt of powder
that makes me a black and white photo—
one taken by Lisa. "A Ballerina Prepares."

The Pain

When he left, you cried.
A week after he left, you cried.
A month, a year after, you cried some more.

The pain of loving, the pain of living, the pain of breathing and of sleeping, the pain of not sleeping, they are acute and dreadful tortures; hellish cuts scarring the milky skin.

How would you live without your soul?

He was the source of your anger and my elation. He was your pleasure and your pain.

Once upon a time there was a Russian boy and an American girl, and he left her to return to his war torn country.

You remember giving your life away, the lot of womanhood, and then not remembering what to do with it when it was returned.

"Now is Portia time," your mother would say. She was right, of course, but you didn't want "Portia time."

You wanted him.

You wanted to fight with him, to throw things at him, to cry to him, to have him dispel your fears, to have him tell you to ignore everyone else because they all "sucked!"

Time rushed by, and life rushed by.

You barely lived. You remember living. Your living was a haze of experience, waking up in the morning, drinking coffee, listening to music, watching television, eating lunch, eating dinner, running here, there and everywhere, aimlessly running.

You remember doing things, forcing yourself to do things. In fact the year and a half after he left were probably among the most productive years of the 28 you had been alive.

You were a ballerina before he came; you belonged to him when he was here, and you were a ballerina once again after he left.

A photographer friend clicked, clicked, clicked endlessly one Sunday afternoon.

Ballerinas take pretty pictures; heartbroken ballerinas take exceptional pictures, your soul imprisoned within your small frame, your pain transparent in black and white photographs.

"Narcissistic nausea" should have been the title of her work.

You are too severe.

She was right.

They *were* beautiful photographs, the romantic aspect of longing illustrated by your breathing organism.

Unfortunately, you find nothing romantic about being unhappy, even when the unhappiness is garbed in billowy, white tulle.

At 26, a week before Tagir left, you went to see your ballet teacher and private coach, pictures of long dead ballerinas in their prime scattered throughout her office.

"What happened to you?" she asked, for you had disappeared from that life only two years before, not wanting any part of it.

"I fell into one of those holes in life, and I couldn't get out," you told her. "I didn't know what else to do with myself, so I ran here."

She smiled and was understanding.

"I do that too when life gets too tough. Just start from 2nd position," she said.

Her words helped.

You needed to go on; you needed to feel something,

anything.

You knew that ballet would consume your life and absorb your desperation and loneliness.

He saved you from yourself when he became your friend; he made you want to live; now you had to go on without him.

Distraction became salvation.

You worked, worked, worked.

You returned to a life of bloody feet, cramping arches, and sweat, yet you felt nothing, nothing, nothing.

You started going into Manhattan again, the 7:46 out of Stony Brook station, morning commuters everywhere, the pain of no sleep, the pain of coldness and fatigue.

You took your morning class with American Ballet Theatre. "Ballet is ballet is ballet," you thought to yourself. "Does anyone really care about toe shoes and tutus?"

There were always flashes of Tagir in Russia, flashes of life, real life, taunting you, a life where people lived, where they worried about substantial things.

He lives with bombings in Moscow, with a war in Chechnya.

You felt little and pathetic walking through Manhattan, sitting on the train, the good old LIRR.

He would call you from Moscow, and it was painful to talk to him, the line between the pleasure and the pain was blurred.

You hurt from loving him.

You hurt from missing him.

You hurt from wanting him to be happy.

You hurt from wanting to be happy yourself.

"They consigned us Chechens to Siberia during the second world war," he said. "The Russians seem to think they're Europeans with their obsession for pure blood; they're dumb these people. They'll never be European."

He was always so tactful.

"There's a war going on Tagir," you would say into the telephone, laughing with happiness at the sound of that voice, that palpable, liquid voice you adored, yet miserable at the distance separating that utterance from you.

"War nothing. It's genocide baby!!!"

You felt insignificant and spoiled.

"I want to hear everything about you. What are you doing? Are you dancing?" he would ask.

You would tell him that you were, and he would be happy.

You would tell him that you had no idea why you were dancing, what you were trying to achieve. Purpose was lost to you in the melding of pain and confusion.

He understood that feeling.

He lived with that feeling daily.

Sick uselessness.

Flashes of Maria Callas watching "I Love Lucy" with a troubled student would permeate your mind at odd moments.

This was one of those moments.

When the episode was over Callas said to her young charge, "Tell me why you can't hit that note. I know you can hit that note. You know you can hit that note. Tell me what's wrong."

"I don't know," the girl replied. "It's just that sometimes I feel so useless. . . ."

Callas paused.

"I feel like that all the time," the disappointed diva responded.

Pain would ease, with the murkiness of his rapturous voice, only to strangle you once again when you returned the phone to the receiver.

A second summer came and went without him.

You danced everywhere; it was a painful, exhausting distraction.

You danced in Finland and were plagued with loneliness.You spoke with him from Helsinki, and you told him you hated him for not coming to see you.

"I can't come see you Portia. I'm stuck in Moscow!"

Even when you hated him you couldn't hate him.

No one knew you the way he did, although you couldn't quite remember who this "you" was anymore.

You lost yourself when you lost him.

You decided to revisit your old ballet school, your old ballet teacher Maria (Russians, Russians everywhere). You hadn't seen her in almost ten years.

Memories of being 16 again flooded your senses like a purple cloud raining in your head.

You laughed and cried at your reunion. You were swept backward into the gallery of ballet; images of Degas and the mysticism of adolescent dreams wafted through the enormous studio.

This was your young life, ballet classes 6 days a week with Maria, summers spent with such and such ballet company and with various teachers who hailed from all over the world.

It was a place for girls who did not like real life. After taking a side turn from the world, they emerged here, in the midst of the hallucination. Here they were safe from adolescence, from boys, from the pain of becoming women.

You did not choose ballet.

It chose you.

As a young mesmerized girl, drifting in the whirlwind of gauzy magnificent women and their adoring cavaliers, you were a willing follower. At 16, you embraced the hazy fantasy with every fiber of your life.

It was black magic.

Somewhere you grew up.

At 24 working with Cara, you peered outside of the ballet studio window, and you saw a world that resembled nothing you knew.

After the near breakdown that ensued, the crying, crying, crying that wouldn't stop, you left.

You wanted to join that world, seen only through studio windows, that distant, untouchable, unfamiliar place, and Tagir was there.

"What have you been doing kid?" she asked you, hugging you so that you could barely breathe.

"I danced Maria. I went to a private teacher, performances all over the place, modeling."

Silently you mused to yourself, looking at the next generation of young girls being indoctrinated into the dream of a life beyond life.

"All this work exists for nothing," your soul screamed.

It's a distraction for a small audience.

Yes, that is important you suppose, but it wasn't enough for you.

You wanted to create something tangible.

People read books and fall in love and drink hot chocolate! For you, that was living.

Upon seeing her again, the pain of inspiring any disappointment vanished.

A piece of self-loathing evaporated.

You thought she would hate you for wanting more.

She didn't.

She loved you still.

One winter day, after Tagir had been gone for over a year, after you had nearly collapsed from exhaustion, you took a class with a small ballet company in Manhattan.

The Artistic Director hated you, hated you, hated you

with a vengeance. You were more disgusted and annoyed than hurt.

You found her laughable.

You snidely thought to yourself, "oh please," as she was hurling insults at you. "I've trained and worked with some of the greatest people in the world. I've given my life to an art that thinks nothing of its artists, where you are only as good as your last performance, and then quickly forgotten. You must be joking."

What had this woman done with her life and why should you care or be impressed?

She had nothing.

Sadly she probably knew that.

You at 26 had learned something she had yet to realize at forty-something.

You walked out.

Fuck her, and fuck this.

You saw her for the miserable, washed-up, nothing that she was, and you were glad to be free.

You were through.

That day, you walked your 5 or so blocks to Penn Station.

Snow was falling.

People were scattering.

You just walked.

You took the train home.

Staring out the white washed window his voice came.

You heard Tagir.

He was speaking in your ear; you could feel him breathing. "What's the matter baby?" he said.

Hot breath soothed you.

"Nothing," you heard yourself whisper.

"If you don't tell me, I can't help you baby." His voice

was probing and little. "Are you tired?"

He was mocking you, teasing you in his usual way.

He knew how to make you talk.

The pain of familiarity, of the rich sound of his voice ringing in your ear made you convulse.

"No," you said to the invisible voice in your head. "I'm anything but tired."

You heard him inhale, deeply.

You couldn't hear the train.

When the conductor asked for your ticket, you were in a daze. You were cold, and you were wet, yet the clamminess didn't saturate you.

There was only his voice, and the muted life around you, and snow falling outside the window.

When the conductor complemented your black fur hat, you mechanically thanked him and managed an appreciative smile.

"He thinks you're beautiful baby," Tagir laughed at you. "Didn't you notice that? Are you blind?"

"No Tagir, I'm not blind. The complement was very sweet."

"You know baby, I worry about you sometimes."

"You worry about me," you were agog.

"Damn straight. Don't let them poison you. You have everything. If people give you a hard time, tell them where to go. God knows you have no problem telling me where to go!"

"That's different Tagir."

"Oh really!"

Suddenly you wanted to live without him.

You needed to live without him.

Sadness choked, choked, choked you, and you wanted that pain to vanish.

"I'm sorry," you whispered to that invisible voice in your head.

"Why?" he asked.

"Because I wish I never knew you. I hate you for leaving me here. I hate that I still miss you. I hear you all the time talking to me, and I want your voice to go away."

You could feel him kiss your cheek and squeeze your hand.

He was lovely.

He was as real to you as the hat you wore.

You felt him all the time.

"I'm not dead Portia," he said, mimicking his own accent, emphasizing the long sound of the "r" in your name. "I'm still here. You can't get rid of me."

You closed your eyes and went to sleep.

You reached home and cried, cried, cried.

Somewhere you learned to live with those tears, with that pain, and life somehow became easier. They became a constant, and you knew they would never leave you, completely.

You cried because you knew you'd cry less.

In The Cut

Razor slashes register
my life, in blood—

in marks on a page
so white—my flesh,

like the petals of an orchid,
speckled and flecked

with my daily walking,
my daily musings.

You are always present—
in me—in the blood,

in the cut that you
did make. I bleed

you on those
flowers as I inhale

their perfume,
their serenity. That

peace is heady and lost
to me, in the undercurrent

of your possession,
which is now my life.

Alert Senses

In that swirl of
coffee, I swim, daily—
searching for
the vibrant awakeness,
that upright
coil of acuteness,
that leads me away,
and to, thoughts of
you—imbued with
a majesty, sublime
and colored
by the alert senses
underscored always by
dreams of
the day I'm going
away, sadly.

Cotton Stuffed

You were there—
then came separation—silence—
their cotton stuffed faces.
Then, you here—cold, steely
clockworks ringing your despair.
Dry and aching, your lips blossomed,
like my imploring embraces.

Spirit—slighted
horizontally, in mold they eat—us—
those boys now living in the ground.
Life—elusive and empty is
pockmarked and blighted.
Made wretched I am, not caring if
they ever make another sound.

Beseeching you not to leave me—
in patchiness blue—
and abandon—me, here.
You are now wrecked far away
in an abyss—
where in mire-clogged shoes you
cannot be found—you— life, an ignited crack bouquet.

That thick, espresso-twinkling capacity
of your eyes, sickly blighted orbs—
Chechen
and ravaged are you—
With bold audacity
you inhale, recalcitrant, cocksure,
but mention

my name, quietly—
somewhere in your
obliterated mind,
smacked by death
and the demented visions—of hardcore
filth and—loving.
There's no baby's breadth

for flowers, pink roses or white,
the ones I love.
You remember? Me, Stealing Beauty
alone, yes still— I'm
here, awake—impatient for your sound,
not devoid of
that molasses, horizontal lilt.

It's no war crime
to repeat my name—here, two blocks
from Moscow
with an ocean in between, I believe—
Masters and Margaritas I detest in spite
of you—Pretty books in a row
are like the boys—our dead,
suffocated fasters.

In silence—amazing,
now am I, like those dead boys
alone, writhing and waiting.
Wanting you here, I breathe in a river.
A wet engraving
is my cheeks—painful aching for your
thick warm
black—eyed gazing.

That Frontier

When did the world
become the bottom
of my coffee cup?
For me—never. Life
lives, this American
world, where there is the red smear—the
frontier—Go west young man—
I heard it cried,
crying, in the dirt
where they died, and
that is my life—still—
the richness of
it all—no more
undrinkable.

Green Washes

Green washes in
April, are
like the hills

of our school—in
summer—far
away—It fills

my hands. A kin
of my starring
sky, it wills

my breadth—breathing
hard, my sparring
mate—so mills

my mind. Slow in
action—are
tears, the ills

of attaching—to
me. Your star
is my killer.

It calls me home.

Through The Windows

Through the windows of our
schoolroom the light was
always slanted,

prism-like slices that made
snug the tiled floor, and
left me,

in polished shoes, gazing
at something, my blindness.
I was

always naïve. They were
like the windows at ABT,
through

which I looked daily—
at the world, at life
absent

from my own. The *Seeing*
came again. It stretched
through my woman's eyes,

once hazy little girl eyes,
sleepy and wanting mommy,
not you,

definitely not you—sitting
behind me, with that voice
that never goes

away. Still today, I hear it.
Blue jeans and white
tee shirts

were the sound—American boys,
jocks in waiting, airmen
in training.

I didn't like knowing
you—ever, especially
then. A Cheshire Cat.

You scared me with
the silent aspect, the
raven blue

echo in your whiteness,
Nazi pallor—it was so ivory,
through

that sunlit prism of early
Stony Brook mornings
that morphed

into afternoon train
rides from Penn Station,
when rehearsals

began, and I, all grown up,
went home to assuage
my tired feet.

Like The Floss

When I was a child, I spake as a child
or I didn't speak at all—I know you didn't.

You could never talk, and I liked that,
the silence washing over, yet words

words, always milling under your gentle
coolness, sublime and sand cracking,

like the Floss, the river in that book
I hated, then loved when I grew up, at

least I thought I did—grow up, elegant
and graceful—the Cheshire said. Is there a remnant

of me in me, from then, from littleness
when I chattered high pitched, before

my voice went low, like yours—now? Yes
I guess we've a call—to not talk—but speak, silently.

Is Yuri still playing, underneath it all?
Is Yuri still playing the upright—something in four—

underneath it all?

At Flag Day

At Flag Day, all red and white, you were there—
      somewhere in the vast Lilliputian

field of *Our Town*. School all brick, yes,
      and red, I remember, but I don't

remember you there. I was small
      and you were tall in jeans—no doubt,

no, not at all—always in jeans and I
      in ribbons and frills—little snotty

girls in curls—with snotty boys, not
      so rare indeed. Is this where love

begins—Maggie and Tom—or misery perhaps?
      Maybe there is a difference—Sun

jets only bounce off of some clean, bright
      prettiness, exact and smooth—like

your little Cheshire hands were—yes
      they were smooth then—before

they could hold a gun—must've been.
      I think mine did fit in yours, slightly.

Orange Petals

Orange petals I hear screaming.
They're searing and parching

under the peachy, fat, moon sighing—
I hear breadth hurting and unyielding—

The tears droop, and I feel
razors slice my eyes—

It's an unwielding glimmer.
I follow. I look, sideways—which way—

Sleeping Beauty, trips me and laughs.
Abandonment, and tentacles of terror, creep, and sway.

But where am I to pass?
Those swirling orbs, black buttons,

like revolvers in my brain—
they're Mommy's black eyed Susans—

They're like me, she says—
drowning in the wet residue

of feral pain and sun and rain,
but now—afterwards, they're softer.

I hear my breath in a mist, newly elected—
and the flowers soothe my skin

as I sleep in the grass.

I Didn't Let You Kiss Me

I didn't let you kiss me—
anytime you wanted—not then, once
on the blacktop—where the
Indians ran, must've run—*Minnsesauke.*
I think it was a tribe,
like our tribe in the field—where the dandelions
                    grew, grew, grew.

Tomahawks raged and well-matched you,
in blistering fights, always fights—
monkey bar swinging—Cheshire sitting
and you—crashing, on clay.
Your face was rouge, sweltered
                    always pale, white with colorless hair,

banshee hair, screaming and
chasing, terrifying—me—but flesh
a reddish smolder
insignificant, littleness under
your tall, rubber sneaker.
Were you red from the running—and from me
                    running after me?

In my cheeks, in the hollow, red
seared, a blacksmith's poker in my face.
It made me scream—like you, loudly
at your father in the white house—
red with you, rouge with you, insane with you
especially on that playground
                    hopscotching or blacktopping—

Card flicking, you and your friends—
Every day, circling the wagons, wheels
of bicycles—mine was yellow—like the coat
I have today, with flowers.
I see the running, running through those woods
(where the man hid) the savage redness
                              and the killing. Thanks for not

slashing my throat—red cheeks still on
my driveway, with you—and I now let you kiss me
whenever you want.
Without the blood—you promise.
"*Women's poetry* is always about blood
And things ripping," I laughed, and you agreed.
                              Even in the tracks of the Indians

at *Minnesauke*, the *Minnesauke Indians*,
running, you're always
running—You were volcanic and splattered
erupting at your father— and Dave was
at the center, like the spokes of my bike.
I guess the blood smeared with me, in the blushes.
                              But nothing ripped between us.

When You Speak

There is a music in
your voice, now, when
you speak.

It was not always
there, in school, when
we talked, barely.

Somewhere the screeching
became a bass—
It engulfs me breadthlessly

when you utter—words.
Now I listen—the tone
as deafening as

your silence, as invigorating
as an ocean, where I
remember a boy

drowned—as infectious
as Hamlet's ear poison that killed
another one summer—Do you

remember him? His
voice is in a grave, another one
swallowed—Maybe he consumed

me too in the darkness,
like your voice does now, a man's.
I believe I'll die there, mercifully.

"Believe"

Your judgmental eyes look
deep—and through me to
a horizontal nook

in my brain to a new
life, about which
I only dream.

Don't be harsh, witch!
Your sad Greek stream
flows through me,

slicing like a razor.
"I feel Useless."
See. I know what you meant.

My internal maze or
a snuggly blanket for
my tattered blaze

of energy to fold within
—It's a haze sublime,
not measured, like my

daily walk to Broadway and 19th.
I need. But the friction hurts.
Tethered, I feed a desire cut

in my dress with abandon.
Off the sidewalk, and
outside Penn—

She's there, daily, on a
billboard—with those operatic eyes.
"Believe." I hear that voice.

But La Callas has
evaporated--with
my daily tendus.

Transparent Cylindrical Outlines

Sounds ringing my stomach are Like my conjoined twin.
It's an aching, painful desire, inside—deep.

But all for what! I want more, more, more. More of my adrena-
line saturation— I think, that pushes, pushes, pushes

but underneath, it's really just an empty hole, and there's
nothing, nothing left, but a satiated mole.

My baby feet, now, need damage control.
Monsieur, with your cain, spinning outlines on the floor—

Transparent cylindrical outlines—those invisible lines you make
are my toes—against the grimy, wooden,

floors—my morning metronome, I make them again and again—
They trace my heavy woes, My sadness, my frustration

That I see everyday in the mirror of the studio,
Every day in the bottom of my white round coffee cup.

Those circles are my strife, the wars and rages
That repeat in transparent cylindrical outlines

Day in and day out, against myself. Orange Freed's, satin shoes
with ribbons wrapped tightly around my white ankles,

with a bone that bulges, through my white stockings,
Then flashes of old men sewing—they work as hard as I do—

day in and day out to make my ballerina feet beautiful—
but horrible beads of toe shoe agony

distort my baby skin. "I made you beautiful" my mother says—
of a devout worship, of a mythology, sideways

painted, am I the victim? A gallery of Degas—that's me.
Day in and day out, a little girl fantasy, tutus and rouge,

crashes under Chopin's harsh dictum—start from second posi-
tion.The music that plays in circles, Yuri at the piano—smoking,

allusions abounded in my brain-washed beehive—Images were
provoked of a life more ethereal, than my painful feet.

Sculpted old ladies, with sticks in hand—breathing and smoking
more, more , more as my clammy sweat bleeds from my

porcelain pores, clogged with that adrenalin.
Annointed by Diaghilev's fat chin, I thrive under music,

the rhythm, metrical, pounded and belted on that damn
upright—Again, day in and day out, like the old men sewing my

life into my shoes. Day in and day out, do the outlines—
transparent cylindrical outlines, appear on the floor.

The marley of the studio with huge windows and mirrors—
By the barre, the ballet barre—I grip and release—

my shellacked anchor, tight against the wall. My hands never
splintered—I'm Lot's crumpled wife. Grotesque make-up, and

pink tulle slashes of shadow on my eyes bleed relentlessly. My
scarred lashes, under beauty's breathless last thrashes,

reflect my pink soul crashes. And with his fat chin—
in the invisible corner, he sneers, and I hope against hope, in
the static of wanting to be seen.

A Purple Hanger

He sees me
deeply, inside and
under my long
blonde hair—like
Goldilocks—That's
what HE called
me—
And I still smile
at the echo of the
sound—for
the utterance still
exists—somewhere—
hanging in the air,
or on my closet
door. It's draped on
a purple hanger.

My Uniqueness

My uniqueness, in an oxygen crypt
of life and hatred, love and
desire elusive, is pale and
empty, for there is no
singularity—My pulsating soul
drinks
liquid, hot and wet,
from some dogged local
spring—to morph into my
Tagir, Atlantic separated, who
belongs to me—in every
fashion, blind.
My birdie life is vacuous and
vapid—I'm nobody without
you—Who are you? Alone,
but not alone. To find you, my
obscure lover, breathless and
searching,
I live and transfix my satiated flow.
Blood pumped-up, oxygen
bursting, pulsations
emerging, on my white
Virgin sheets—where
Nadja
dreams, and subversive wanderings

find you, staggering, alone, but not alone.
Because I'm in you. Red silk pumps
your being, dark, and angry. My glow is
ignited in your flesh,
extreme.

Like Gretta

I heard music on
that landing,
as Gretta did.

Then came the
reverberation
of Blondie, and who he was, once—

I talk to you
because you knew
him—but not really—

not him with me,
him with you.
You missed his

sweetness, but
I remember it, etched
on the blackboard,

—"Do you read Mad?"
He asked me, and I
didn't know it—

Only Garfield comics
and the cat I drew,
next to his insanity

that said he
would die—in
a few years. The

music was him—and
it lives in me—still
like him now—so still!

I freeze on the landing,
the sound in my ear,
and him, again, repeating—

"Yes I'm here."
I cried in bed, that night
too.

Blondie

I

You once knew a boy, a beautiful boy who sat only two seats in front of you, only two seats, when you were younger, in school.

You remember how you loved him.

Then one day, a few years later, he died.

You felt nothing, nothing, nothing.

You ignored it.

Life rushed on.

II

You drove passed his street every day, yet you still thought nothing. A beautiful all-American boy died one day, and you loved him once.

That was all.

Sensations were dormant. Feelings surrounding him were dormant.

Other horrors of your life came and went; other deaths came and went.

III

One day he returned to you, his death returned to you, the death of the blonde haired boy who sat two seats in front of you, only two seats in front of you, and the crying started, started, and started.

It didn't stop...life changed again, his reverberation, his echo saturated you.

He lived somewhere, and you thought and felt it.

His memory was there, there, and there.

Suddenly, the boy was everywhere, in everything.

IV

You are walking through the halls of a building; it could have been any building, anywhere.

You are 28 years old with long blonde hair.

You hear feet running on the floor above, directly above.

It is as if you are there again, in school, 14 years old. You are no longer the 28-year-old woman. You are somewhere else. You are there, and he is there.

An unknown boy comes running down the stairwell of this building that could have been any building; he runs up behind you and through the doors. He brushes passed you as he runs, and he smiles.

"Sorry," the stranger glows.

Then he's gone.

You know that smile and that look; you stop feeling; you walk sickened and aloof.

You are speechless and confused.

It is as if you are somewhere else.

You are somewhere in a time long gone where a beautiful all-American boy named Paul ran up behind you, and wrapped his arms around your neck to whisper something silly in your ear, something of the all-encompassing love of being 14 and delirious with hopelessness, sweetness, and innocence.

He is just like him, that stranger brushing against you.

He is just like Paul, who sat two seats in front of you, only two seats in front of you, and who died when you were both 18.

You see Paul at 28, and you are lost in a deluge of space splintering against a wall.

V

That was the moment where you realized him.
He was gone.
Now he returned.
Now, now you missed him.
His life bounced off walls, and that evening the crying began,
the crying that you couldn't stop for days and days and days.

"I'm so sorry you're dead and gone," you cried. "I'm
sorry; I'm sorry...."

You now took substantial notice of Gnarled Hollow
Road, every day as you drove under the green light and beyond
the street that led one way to his house, the other way to the
place where he died, while crossing the street one night almost
ten years before.

VI

You hated that he died.
The unfairness sickened you.
Was it really ten years since he died, or maybe almost
ten years?

A car ran him down, ten minutes from your house.
Only ten minutes maybe even five if you sped really fast down
Gnarled Hollow Road, and if you didn't get stuck at that stupid
light.

There he lay in wait of oblivion, off of Gnarled Hollow
Road, two minutes from his house, two minutes from yours.

VII

You keep repeating it, that word, "dead." You hope
and pray that the impact of its meaning will ring inside of you.
The word will develop a life with which you may converse or

with which you may rationalize the irrational.

"Dead."

It has always been a word impossible to process fully.
You say it and say it, hoping that the intensity of its meaning will
become apparent, but it never does.

Death easily takes hold with its quiet simple majesty,
and it sadly leaves you, vacant, abandoned, trying to understand,
succumbing to the state of not understanding and accepting
because you have no choice.

It manages to penetrate gracefully, violently, shockingly.

He was ripped from life, violently ripped to that place of
peace beyond the door.
The God you whispered to when you were 14, ("Does he like
me; I hope he likes me...") you now consult to make certain
that he's all right, that he's not just rotting in a grave somewhere
in the horrible wet ground.

Now, there is only silence for him, an endless silence,
silence, silence for the beautiful blonde haired boy who sat two
seats in front of you and who made your heart flutter when you
were 14 years old.

Now you feel that horrible sadness; the sadness that
makes you want to wretch, the sadness of wanting him to come
back, desperately wanting him to come back. The sadness of
hopelessness, the sadness of uselessness grips you.

The goddamn crying doesn't stop.

You think on his mother and his father.
For almost 10 years they've lived without him, and they
will continue to live without him for another ten or twenty or
thirty years.

VIII

You brought chocolate chip cookies, the richest most
luscious cookies you could find, to lunch because Paul loved

them. You knew how he loved them, and you didn't want him to be disappointed when he came to sit with you, as he did, everyday.

You loved that hour of the day, dreamed of it, waited for it, with palms sweating, with blood rushing. When he came you could barely speak for loving him.

He smiled at you; he gorged himself on the chocolate treat, smeared all over his mouth, and he made you laugh from nervousness, from shyness, from joy at his being near you, sheer, perfect, hopeless joy.

"There he is," your mind whispered. "He's coming over," your mind whispered. You felt the pounding in your chest, and you prayed that you would not die, at least not before he left, or at least not before he teased you, definitely not before he teased you. "Please God," you begged, "Let him come and see me...."

The world would be over.
There would be no life.
There would be no world.
At 14, he was the only boy you swore you would ever love. You were silly and hopeless and horribly shy and embarrassed.

You thought it was lovely, deliriously lovely.
After he died it became bitterly brilliant.
You wished that death could have waited for him.
You're 28 now.

IX

You still think on his smile and you glow; you still think on his posture, and you glow; you still think of his humor, his impetuosity, his perplexity...his impetuosity....

One night he was run down by a car when he ran across a street, off of Gnarled Hollow Road, two minutes from his house, impetuously.

You can see him doing that, standing one moment then suddenly taking off, running.

He would smile of course and laugh, then just take off, impetuously, impetuously; you think of a sprite, a tall blonde haired blue-eyed mischievous sprite playing a trick when you think of his special energy.

A car ran him down, that boy, that beautiful boy who you once loved with all your heart. He lay in the street, dying. Then he was dead.

You wish that you were there. You wish that you could have held his hand when he died in the hospital a few hours later.

X

He took a part of you with him; he took a piece of your childhood, a piece of that innocence and flush of naïve girl-hood. Those aspects of you died with him, that beautiful blonde boy who sat two seats in front of you, the boy who loved choco-late chip cookies, that boy who played basketball and baseball, that boy who innocently mangled your young imagination with the ravages of love.

XI

One evening off of Gnarled Hollow Road, almost ten years ago, the subdued touch of death reached out and grabbed Paul's hand, and left you alive only to remember...and write about him, a dead boy laying in a grave, somewhere.

At 18

He sang to me, lightly
in school, and how

lucky I was to have
been there—those moments,

were so short for him
before he died

at 18—to die at
18. No life really lived.

No love really known,
but maybe it was me—

Love, not between
adolescent sheets,

but in homeroom
and study hall.

Cookies and giggles,
nervousness unchained

like Prometheus Unbound,
only harder, more durable

and residual.
I was there. Yes—and

I'm indebted to have
seen into his youth—

into his beauty, unrealized.
Only fading, fading, fading

was he with only a few
years more to live.

Then the lid closed
and he was inside.

I missed it.
I missed it. I was at ballet.

He's in a snowy field, now
stepped over. No.

He's not alone,
because I was with him then,

and with him
now—still.

My Uncle is buried there too,
with the other soldiers.

I believe his father
was in the Navy?

Cork

Why are you pervasive?
There is a life,
sublime and unruffled
without you
I know—but when
did I know? I don't
remember that time
or place—the clock
in the kitchen
pulsing and beating—
It's a passage
of living—
And you were
always there—unseen

even—but there—
because I believe.
And that clock
ticking is my repose,
as it goes. I know
I radiate daily.
It is life with and without
you—but always
in the undercurrent
that drags me below curling water—

Then I'm popped out
again, like a cork—
but you're still
in me, like the ticking.

Blue North

Will time strip me
        of my beauty and
leave me in seas
        of loss? In ugliness berating

my mind—my true blue
        North? Am I defined
by me? Or by a mirror through
        which I should see myself,

clearly defined?
        What more am I? Nothing.
It's everything plus two—

Alignment in a cosmos internal, and
        does it matter? Yes.
Excavations of her tomb, Nefrititi's

left over life. She's my best guest
        ever, living in the room next door—
and she lives still in beauty,

not obscured in "Cutie Pie" fruit cakes—
        from my boulangerie.
They're gifts of love, of a life lived
        above, on an unearthly shore.

A Pair Of Eyes

Flashes of you and your friend
intervene. A pair of boys
together are like a pair
of eyes so blue.

That was you
and your chum,
your playmate?
Yes, even at 17—

I wondered and
didn't watch—
I didn't care, really,
Sorry, sorry, sorry—

I couldn't get near.
You were too far
and too close—At
17 those two feet

were a mile I had
to walk with
scratched bloody
feet. Ballerina

feet were mine,
uncomfortable without
peach satin and a
ribbon, a poupée

pretty foot, but bare and
soft like a baby.
I never heard
you scream—from the Gulf.

Prokofiev was in
my ear—and no
one taught me
to walk.

Your friend like the piano,
played hard. So I looked
up—
Forgive me.

I Drink Coffee

I drink coffee in the morning
too, black with half and half,
like you do now—but
you didn't before, when we
were little, in school.
It was all milk and juice—
and children things,
kid stuff.
Somewhere you
vanished—
in space—in air. Where?
Sprouting
adultness pervaded.
Its hand insinuated itself.
And you drink coffee,
two cups in the morning now—
but nothing has changed.
Your friend likes half and half—too—
like me.
He has blue eyes like you,
like you.

War Suits You

War suits you, too well, beautifully well,
because, yes, I suppose war
can be beautiful.
Eliot's wars, Hughes' wars—You
wear war better than your own
nakedness—when ironing.

> "You know I iron naked" you said
> in the car—out of nowhere, nowhere, news
> from nowhere.

The heat was your comfort.
The distress was your snug love that
you needed—but the iron?
Did it smite and solder your fingers, long and worn—
Wax the fingers to find the traces, traces, traces

> of the powder—or of my cheek touched
> gently, my hair, curled and smooth.
> "So beautiful."

The loaded gun, the life you
carried. You didn't die—there, naked
and ripped, like the dead you've seen.
But the still silence
in the waiting dead faces was like
your own steely mutation— *(steely like Irina's pirouettes)*

> a station that no one outside could
> recognize, beneath
> the tattoo.

"It's for honor" you said, seated
with me and Dave.

"Did you show her the other one?" Awaiting the silent answer,
he looked at you, and you at him.
Back and forth, back and forth
like the ball toss, when you were eleven at school.

> I was there—too.
> And here again,
> for the new

battle, boyish and constant.
You saw you in the blood pool,
with that blazing metal once pounding your head.
An iron or a gun or a ball or me, who cares?
You'd fix your starched shirts, ironing naked, to talk—
You wore a tie, after, after, after

> you came back, after and before me.
> After the toss, that overlaps, the talk that
> overlaps and the killing.

The you you couldn't leave was you, but you tried.
That you with words—I didn't know him.
On the playground you didn't speak—
The ball, it flies back and forth, back and forth
and Dave catches, then you catch, then Dave
like the ticking of the world.

> Run Forrest Run!
> It was always hot,
> scorching and hideous.

Some leech who inhabited and
drank, devoured your life, your blood—
but gave you a different life—a home—
a warrior's home, finally,
where life vaporizes itself—You were in the Gulf
below the equator, on a sun drenched

> icy desert—that I heard about on the news
> "Don't hit me with that

dodge ball!"

I didn't know you were there—
Thank God—
but did you ever leave? "Run Forrest Run!"
"I've seen a lot of dead people,
and I'm gonna see more," you whispered to me
under beer—"my only vice—I like beer."

Where that left me, I don't know—
in the schoolyard once more—
left behind,

inside of you—scorched,
my breadth sore with you—
always you, like the chocolate Bailey's Dave
gave me when you went away—
"DRINK IT!!!!" It was my Charlie Brown existence
in a moment,

ball back and forth,
back and forth
tick tock encore.

Yet again the scorching and iron in your
gun powdered hands, a combatant grip
once smooth and alabaster,
what happened?
It reverberates, in the toss, through the air, marked
with you—Nothing.

Smooth enough for mine—
your hands, now they are jagged enough
for mine—as well.

You Speak To Me

You speak to me—
devouring my mind
and my haze of mystere.

I breathe in a breadth—now
consigned—to the brevity
of a life unaware of emptiness.

It is loneliness, a
life without you—
extreme abandon, fear—

Je sais pas ce qui se passe
when I hear you—
the words, the sound—

the lilt of the few
moments that arrived—
surreptitiously.

When we speak,
truth shatters glass.
For in perdition, Am I.

My Brain Is A Black Hawk

My brain is a black hawk
downing, itself—

through a sand salted
sky. A smeared mass

of disjointed images,
pastiche-ing and

overlapping, I'm lost in the
winking, winking, winking—

"We've got a black hawk down."

You (breathing)—everything beats,
and Blondie (now dead)—beating again,

always on me, smothering
me—my pillow in which

I cried wet moisture,
from my eyes—black

jewels in their sockets,
the propellers in my brain—

"We've got a black hawk down."

The hard beating and then—
the abrasion falls.

It's all black, with the fall,
and I crash,

hard, and I'm asleep,
with my petal lids

covering those orbs, those black
eyes—that lead.

A Bell Jar Descended

A bell jar descended—and purple distorted
my vision,
>   as was dictated by you—Sylvia—
>   the patron
saint of overachievers. Young women's
depression—
>   your mythology of life—creative life—
>   no matron

can I be, because I write. I live in words—
like you
>   but different. I want to live—not choke under my
>   oblivion,
my silence, my frustration—Can I, can I—dew of
the few
>   flowers on your grave—survive, rightly after
>   the death mission

has not been realized? You are immortal because
you are dead!
>   I don't want black muck breadth—I won't dangle
>   still like
cousin Frances' uncles, five of them in a row—There
is no winged
>   vision of hazy elation—only life beyond degradation.
>   I hike

through tangled seaweed and willows weeping—my
smeared field
>   of vision. Is it like yours was? Doubtful—for I,
>   am near

thirty too, and I still breathe and plan to breathe—more.
Sexiness will not wield
      its seduction through my corpse's whispers—
      Hear

not the essence of my soul—my words, scratched by
breathing finger traces
      on old crumpled paper—tightly stretched in my coffin.
      I'm in the strokes, existing
      beyond and through time's lost spaces.

Purple Plums

I see them—

The purple plums are
in a bowl—near

a pitcher—
a pumped-up jug

reclined, beyond—
the door.

I imbibe the
sweet scent melting—

through him,
in his mouth,

his skin, and I—
want more—
of the plums, he eats—

the solidity,
all juiciness profusion.

Richness congeals—
I taste—

the pulp overflowed
an ecstatic flavor.

The sweet liquid
drips—

a warped delusion.
For he, in rapture

drunk—
dans ma chair—

elated, I implode.

Down The Steps

I left that studio
and never looked backwards
or sideways—
It was easy—so easy—too easy
to walk away,
down the steps of Penn
and onto the train.

"I don't want it. I don't want it"
Reverberated—like the wheels on the track,
then the numbness came—
the frozen sorbet—that brain
mortar that made me
blind and numb,
I was frozen again—
but high pitched.

I was free.

Emma's Black Bile

When I, life congested, die—
will my failure—plague
and eat me?

A dreamy land fill
for my bones—vague
and nebulous—

will be my lackluster stony grave.
I'm a slave of—buzzing
bees—a wispy saliva

rave—like Emma's Black Bile indiscretion!—
Her white
wedding gown is stained.

A funeral mile
is walked—Me
and a mite,

laugh at my harsh
rejections—but no one
in future will despair,

know—or care—In a dry marsh
will sleep—my lost
willful, sprightly, flare.

In Clod-Like Blunders

In clod-like blunders
      my feet thud
      through black mud
heavy—asunder

the 500-ton tower
      on my light ice-cream
      hair—that screams
and howls.

I am, I am, I am
      is my heart beat.
      The words are sweet
and haunt—The petals slam

me. They slyly whip
      and slash my pink senses.
      Confusion—defenses
are erect—and clip

my courage. I am, I am,
      in a footstep's rhythm and rhyme—
      through mud, crimson, with my time
on earth, almost gone. Slam!

The mud weight pounds.
      I am, I am, I am—tick.
      The metronome does beat quick—
and rhythm sounds.

Again and again
      I force myself
      to walk with stealth—
a viola's refrain

from regulation practice—
      Metronome lashes
      of me, ink slashes
on paper—Bach's life in this,

in the mud, my feet
      thick-soled-clogging—
      I am—flogging—
I am, I am—beat—
      in the grave. Are my
      feet, neat?

Years pass, and he's still dead.

Ice Cream Straws

We lived and we walked
you and I,
hand in hand, once
upon a time,

in a land far away—the
crack came and the
world divided,
the abyss, serrated

and wedged with
agony—
My mother's ice cream
through a straw—

drips into that well.
We stepped
away, but someone
fell—you—I fear.

Hold my hand, now
again.
Skip, skip, skip,
hopscotch and football,

"I played ball" you said,
and you did.
I was there. I know—and
we held hands?

Not quite.

You were never that
one, the sweet one—
You fell, again, but

this time, I finally
caught you—
in a way.

Then I turned
away—but you
left me first!

The Movie Plays

There is a radiance of
the mind—glaring
and speckled in
its apple core

brilliance—It is
the luster
beaming in your
hallucinatory

eyes, globes—throbbing
irretrievably in
my mind—Stop please.
The movie plays—

pictures flashing
gaping holes that
were my life with you
and without you— and plays

an Olympic marathon.
Then the trip, the fall—
stabbing forward—to me, with daggers,
you sliced my neck—

It's your conquest,
your eradication
of me, that completes
my compulsories—

I felt that
gun explode, and it did
hurt, sincerely.

You were in the desert?

Our Stairs Are Dark

Our stairs are dark with the
clack, click— click clack

of my shoes on their nightly watch.
Spanish steps stick In my cheek. I taste hues

Of your love, chic and red, and
I'm no longer dead. I'm Lady Lazarus.

"With my gin, I take peaches and cream."
My new life, my new world,

My new everything—where voices
change and faces—all commedia—smile

and laugh.
A birdie buzz—chirps in delicious dankness—

then comes the clack, click- click clack
of the baby's rattle, in the park where I sat—

It ate my skin, the sound, the buzz
the rattle. The friction incited my pain,

jolted my energy, ALIVE, like that short of measured gin.
"I take peaches and cream" I tell the bartender.

Then I sip. I drink warm and neat with you again.
"Thank you."

Your fresh scent I loved—like that baby, rank

with pleasure for the rattle, like the one I lost—

somewhere on the steps, in the dark—
My core shakes, like pink rocks

who like dancing Spanish tangos in shady
closed places, romantic with a Siamese twin.

Can you dance with me? Like
the pebbles in the rattle that he shakes,

the baby—so warm, bright and ecstatic?
You know my dizzy craze—our intricate phrase.

Here are my shoes. Stuff your feet inside.
But they've changed. They don't fit me anymore.

My once ballerina feet, are now bound and Chinese.
It's a dance I do not know.

Again I taste gin, warm and neat while
sitting on the steps. It tastes like Sunday once more.

Then that BUZZ rings true.
The birdie chirp, flirting with me and the

pink rattle, so silent, sits on the stair.
Searching, I'm lost, with the

clack, click- click, clack of heels on wood—
a sound I do not know,

A darkness I cannot see. Where's my rattle?
It's so far away!

And I'm bound inside these damn shoes—

Tight and unfamiliar—I'll never make it

to the landing, through the
darkness and the buzz, the birdie buzz—

faded and tired, I sit on the step. Hung over—
"It's time to go back to the convent."

In my red dress, I wait—I just need a minute.
I'm too tired, unable to move,

save for my reach to the rattle,
now in my hand, secure.

About Marina Tsvetaeva

Marina's piano song—
     pounds! Harsh!
in my ears—for long
     waxy, clogged, breeches

Of time—Black,
     purple measures wage
Click, click clack—
     like a musical rhythmic sage.

Do you try to force words, ringing
     sublime?
And still—in ink slashes—stinging,
     you mime

silently, from a grave.
     Black, quicksand, again—
Your shadow, Queen Mave
     of Moscow, must—sustain

me, here—still in a mire—lost—
     Drowning, in love's heavy cost.
Like your blue-faced hanging
     is my heart's dismal panging.
Which way do I go?

A Hollow Man

He was going to die,
and I wouldn't know the
truth until
after, after, after,
the coffin was closed,
the ground was broken,
and he was tucked away—

in that hollow cavity.
He was a hollow man—
T.S. Eliot—*("He went to the Sorbonne too")*
might have known him
narrowly, from the corner
of his adept eye—
all seeing, sensing slightness.

Do they know
the hollow became your home?
Is he hollow in that
tooth cavity?—Now filled,
he took a slice of my
hollowness, with him—
I must remember to visit,

and I'll bring some cakes.

Because Of Me?

You said you did it
because of me,

but I doubt it, hard
and succinctly and

purposefully, yes.
Upside down and backwards,

I know it's not true.
You couldn't see—and

that's when you jumped
over the coil, tight and

unsprung, through that
wall of energy leading you somewhere—

that vapid space—like you said
they were—those girls.

But you were never near me.
Couldn't be—

I didn't live there—
in that negative hollow

where you dwelt.
It was Ecstatic Orange

like Heather and Jock at NYCB--
orange Freed's and insects bending--

It made
your eyes severe and

sadistic and you hated—
always, reviled—

everything—but yourself
most of all—

The Web Toile

Did you wait patiently
long for it?

The crash—the damage,
or more drawn out agony—longer.

Maybe there is a slice fate inscribes
somewhere, in your wit's

hard drive—
Or maybe it just slices

the web *toile* of your
thinking, a labyrinth of

connection, the Long Island Power Grid
to which you were tied,

and charged.
Black and stringy the

web was, on the day you
chose, chose—how did you *decide?*

Or did you slant your triangle brain
to make it happen?

Confusion dined in your senseless gate.
The power blew—

again in September, with you.

Naked Thought Is Rampant

Naked thought is rampant in
life—lived, death
waiting in haunted repose.

Phosphorescent lovers
—endure in paper cups,
crumpled—empty and morose.

Attending my other prong
—I have
in silence cried—

stuffed and stifled
with soaked yearning—I am
un esclave

of time—but no—
I speak unmuffled
to him. He hears me

—blue and clear,
and I the words become
—no more trapped by fear.

Rabid Doses

In rabid doses
      of mutilated emotion,
bleeds my psychosis,
      my turgid ocean

of depthless dark feeling.
Love swelling and reeling

is painful.
But I need you,

out of the dark tides.
      Through the mired
wetness you abide
      my hard fired

misery.
In loneliness

is my aching, blearing
fission searing.

When I hear you
      muted, wandering through the
murkiness pure,
      I scream, silent, "Find the key"

to Me.
I'm not so far

away, after all. With the proper vision,
transluscence simplifies your mission.

Take the Robitussin
        and cough me out!
I'm in your bile--an orange
        ribbon by Freed,

trapped and caught
in your rough hands.

Dorothy And Toto

Our school is still
up the street
from my house—

Dorothy and Toto
ran and skipped
there once, to school—

but you didn't smile
by this time. A father
dead and a friend

distraught under
a heavy hand, and
you were troubled too—

In a shirt with
writing—always—
It was on the wall

like a magic spell
scrawled on your heart.
She ran and skipped

and met the magician—
Who? You again, and
again—I close my eyes

And click my heels.
I'm home, but where?

Without you? Is that

The place? Click and skip—
The dog follows—more steps
in my imagination,

and there's a
balloon ride
too, no doubt.

Mona Lisa

You ran outside, in the chill
of the air to help. She had so
many packages, brown wrappings
pouching cakes and milk and bread
so white, so soft, like your
skin—the petal-ness I loved
to touch—silky and warm—
Your face tried but couldn't
conceal flaccid
worries, worries, worries,
always there,
concerned traced in your brow.
I followed you—
to help, help, help you,
and you
simply smiled. Mona Lisa
kissed your mouth—and you said,
"I know you're cold. Go inside."

In The Darkness

In the darkness—
I saw you wink

and smile, a
crooked endeavor

first—to me, always
give your pink

blinding stare, in a
maze forever.

I'm nobody!
Just a wisp of

alabaster ice-cream.
Who are you?

In your black throated hurt—
With Abysmal voices

you whisper through
my dream.

Tell me you will live,
here, not in the dirt.

Don't wait for my
birdy hands—tender,

to excavate the ground
where you will lay—not yet.

Behind The Door

Everything that is
not you disappears
every night
behind the white
creamy door of
my bedroom—
I see your face,
two times, yours
and his—both
as one, indiscernible
and ravishing—
burning in my
blindness, my white
unseeing—We're
alone in that space
under my covers,
and it's not as
dark as before,
yet darker.

Sitting Quietly

Sitting quietly, trying to
read or live—beneath and above
the thoughts,

ringing, ringing, ringing
I see you, as always.
You pervade and haunt

like a dangling thread—
Holly Golightly's Cat playing
incessantly—and I cannot

stop the temptation
to think, think, think
of you.

The sadness of your
vacancy—
comforts me uniquely.

Rouge Colored

Rouge colored flowers swelter in summer,
in streaks of blazing sulfur—

Delight emerges, under you.
I, in greedy slumber, feel the essence,

the night fright of virgin dreams,
hesitant and longing—

Stay, stay, stay! I desire to shout, but
it's a muffled voice—mine, in murkiness.

Thronging dreams, I have of you—
out of the black unruffled window—

as Septimus plunged—spike inhaled
through the air. That's me—

I'm so bizarre and jigsaw, but you see me alone—
life assailed and weak. You help me stand.

No arctic char, scratching my little
girl ribs, will mar my clear vision,

altered by words or hesitation.
Throw it away— Life—like he did,

out the window—thud—a mission
for freedom. The bones cracking are

like my dismay—cracking under your
flesh. A light revision flashes your blue eyes—

blinding me—In submission washing deeply,
I lay. "Dalloway, Dalloway."

Ashes of your life haunt—but no.
A new, virile rendition assuages.

Out the window, he jumped.
So did you—so did I—in

girl's white sashes, crisp and clean,
for we know the truth that the dead did sow.

Southern Comfort

You were never cruel,
at least not really—
not like Tagir—

With residue in his throat,
residue of Moscow and Chechnya,
killing the "Russian way."

No. That was never you.
That hardness, yours, was
unique— American, eyes and smiles—

always. Boyish, with strokes
of worldliness—the malice
of maturity that you

cannot know—Please
stay on the porch, in the
green lawn chair, in

sneakers and jeans—Your
scrubbed jadedness
is my southern comfort.

Sundrops

I've yet to see
sundrops on your

face—
It's always

shaded,
brightly by

your constant
focus. An election

of elders
sits there, in

the furrow of your
concentric brow.

Steel Girders

Great steel girders
with wind blowing in and through—
a Master And Commander
sail, with flecks

of water overwhelming—
wet and saturating,
it's my pity—my grog,
my Bailey's or my White Russian—

He was white, so pale and pallid,
like mom's whipped cream
on chocolate pie—like the sail,
Master And Commander, where

Aubrey laughed, "lucky Jack."
Now, now, now,
he's a sailor's brother.
You. Adieu to "Red Oktober."

Is the same Russian zeal under the
Arctic, under the waves
where your brother went overboard?
and the girders—again—

Steely is your iciness—
hard in the stinging water,
splashing my pastel face
that finally

reverberates—
all peachy and awake at last.

Pearls

Why does your
brow undulate—such
living--

drawn there, when your
father died?
Pearls were in

his eyes,
doubtless, like
they are in yours,

nightly. They're the
eyes I see in the dark,
penetrating my espresso

night. It's a necklace
of pearls. Gloria Morgan
chewed them,

and now the beads
entangle my feet,
wrapping my

toe shoes--
together.
I'm en pointe.

Complacency

It falls like sprinkles
of rain—your

complacency, lightly
always, so that I

can maneuver
myself, underneath—

again, underneath you—
Your will, your thumb

is in my mouth. Was
that my babiness revisited?

Or was it just you,
in me—my mind, my

thoughts, pierced
over and over—and

sodden—like that
charging water—now heavy

on me. You drench me,
leaving me soggy

and altered, but
with the storm eruption

comes the anxiety—
Yes your thumb is in

my mouth—We're little,
but not so little, because

I can taste the lye on
your finger.

Deux Pas

A deux pas de chez moi—
A deux pas de chez toi—

Est-ce mon existence vrai?
Je crois, oui puis non,
quand la lumière est froide
ma vitesse clair—sublime

mais tu est la, toujours.

C'est toujours—deux pas de chez toi,
en même temps,
dans la même espace variée.
C'est toujours—deux pas de chez moi.

Et je respire,
tranquillement, dans ma vie,
et la lumière
encore froide, mais maintenant

sutile comme toi—
justement deux pas,
seulement deux de chez toi—
ma vie, ma tristesse—

Tu est la—enfin.

Supple Whispers

When I think of you standing
there, you're never alone,
because somehow I'm with
you—under your skin,
under my clothes,
lingering long and in supple
whispers, in the warmth
and cold of the air—
There's a breadth, another and another,
that you breathe, and I'm in
that air—vibrant, cutting, cool
and real. Am I your life as
you are mine?

Your Timidity

Your timidity
is my breadthlessness, fine
and pure. I'm ballooning—again.
A slender balloonist
am I, with tapered fingers
reaching, always—
to you across the
way, the room, the sofa,
our bed—
soft and clean.
I'm saturated with
your scent—
It's my oxygen, and
I can barely breathe—
in and out, in and out,
in the air. From my basket
I'm falling—
with the grip of your
breadth, my breadthlessness—
in my throat.

Nothing Is Left

All I live for is
you, or at least
that is the
incarnation of
my senses,
smeared and
heated, always
heated, a tension
wire chemical
stirring in my
head. Nothing is
left of me,
when I see you.

Diaghilev's Debrief

A dilettante is not an Akhmatova—So divine was she. "Recite
the Rosary."
I wish I was there, next to her, with her dark hair pinned back,
so elegantly—

Like Giselle—my Giselle, deceived yet forgiving—reborn and
enduring.
No drama, no death-like smears of white tulle draping my pale
body—

But wait, Anna's gone. And I am left to painfully
undress—
such pretty changing rooms at the Met—to disrobe
seductively.

Where am I in the jigsaw? "Recite the Rosary," plays again, that
chant
from a Moscow Bar—ugly and horizontal. I hear voices in other
rooms.

They search for words—but I hear my silence speak. On little
bird crutches am I,
A Lilliputian Ballerina—once and still—I fumble hard to my
commander in chief—

"Start from second position," as Cara said—way back—
years ago.
I still listen. Like I now listen to the sound of your voice—"Give
me a Kiss."

The metronome of my everyday—day in and day out, the com-

forting sound is
So real to me—more real than the shoes on my feet, rosin-caked
and

discarded—"You're prettier when you keep your mouth
shut."
It was always easier not to speak—to the dead—to Cheshire
Puss—to you.

Bang, flash—I go back and forth, white sand and the
Cheshire,
Bang, flash—Dorothy and Toto—walking to school, running to
catch up.

The radiance overwhelms, and it's my turn to go down the
floor—
When the music starts again, I go. At the end—in the corner
HE waits.

And I wait too—still silent and breathless—for
Diaghilev's Debrief.

Fin

Further Reading

Winter Season
By Bentley

Dancing On My Grave
By Kirkland

Holding Onto The Air
By Farrell

Speaking Of Diaghilev
By Drummond

Edgar Degas: Dancers And Nudes
By Schacherl

The Collected Poems Of Anna Akhmatova
By Akhmatova

Ariel
By Plath

The Diary Of Vaslav Nijinsky
By Nijinsky

Diaghilev's Ballets Russes
By Garafola

The Picture Of Dorian Gray
By Wilde

The Complete Poems Of T.S. Eliot
By Eliot

About The Author

Portia Franco is Christina Tumminello, niece of novelist Robert Leuci. She is a retired American ballerina, having studied with American Ballet Theatre, The Finnish National Ballet, and the Eglevsky Ballet. She was further educated at *L'Universite de Paris IV, La Sorbonne* and at *Yale University,* as well as holding an MA in English and European Literatures from *C.W. Post College at Long Island University.* Her fiction has appeared in *Fiction International, Babel Magazine* and *Paradoxism.* In addition to authoring various essays, she has published translations of the classic French novels *The Princesse of Cleves* by Madame de La Fayette and *Manon Lescaut* by Abbe Prevost.

Printed in the United States
89664LV00001B/66/A